HURRY UP,
SLOWPOKE

Andrew

Hildebrand
is 5 years old

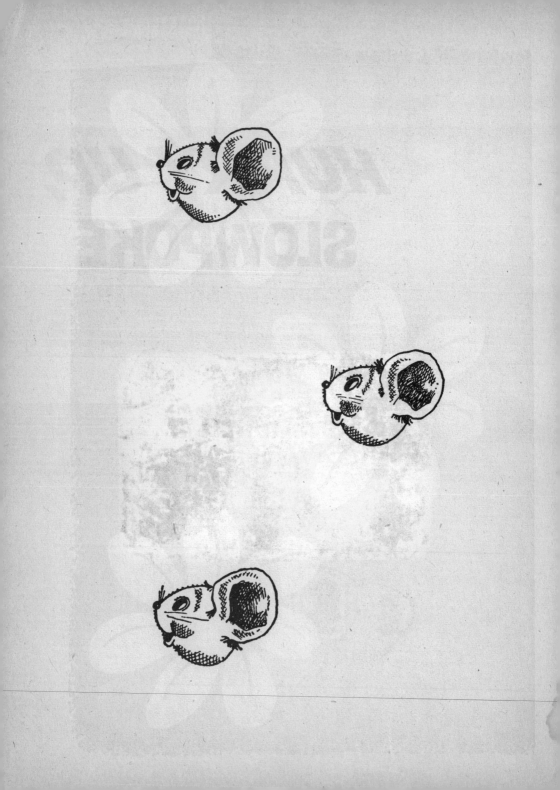

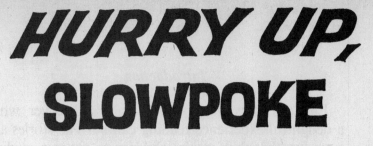

HURRY UP, SLOWPOKE

Written and Illustrated by
CROSBY NEWELL

Editorial Consultant
LILIAN MOORE

Wonder® Books
PRICE/STERN/SLOAN
Publishers, Inc., Los Angeles
1986

Introduction

Easy Readers help young readers discover what a delightful experience reading can be. The stories are such fun that they inspire children to try new reading skills. They are so easy to read that they provide encouragement and support for children as readers.

The adult will notice that the sentences aren't too long, the words aren't too hard, and the skillful repetition is like a helping hand. What the child will feel is: "This is a good story—and I can read it myself!"

For some children, the best way to meet these stories may be to hear them read aloud at first. Others, who are better prepared to read on their own, may need a little help in the beginning—help that is best given freely. Youngsters who have more experience in reading alone—whether in first or second or third grade—will have the immediate joy of reading "all by myself."

These books have been planned to help all young readers grow—in their pleasure in books and in their power to read them.

Lilian Moore
Specialist in Reading
Formerly of Division of Instructional Research,
New York City Board of Education

Copyright © 1961 by Price/Stern/Sloan Publishers, Inc.
Cover Copyright © 1981 by Price/Stern/Sloan Publishers, Inc.
Published by Price/Stern/Sloan Publishers, Inc.,
410 North La Cienega Boulevard, Los Angeles, California 90048

ISBN: 0-8431-4310-X

Wonder® Books is a trademark of Price/Stern/Sloan Publishers, Inc.

"Come, now," said Mrs. Mouse,

"we are going to see Grandmother."

Lucy Mouse put on her hat.

Simon Mouse got his coat.

Simon said, "Lucy, your hat

is upside down."

Lucy gave her hat a little pat.

"It is not," said Lucy.

"It is so," said Simon.

"Is not," said Lucy.

"Is so," said Simon.

"Not," said Lucy.

"So," said Simon.

"CHILDREN!" said Mrs. Mouse.

"Simon, put your coat on."

"Yes," said Lucy.

"Simon, put your coat on."

Mrs. Mouse said,

"We must not be late."

"No," said Lucy,

"we must not be late."

"I'm coming," Simon said.

"Well, hurry, then," said Lucy.

"You are a slowpoke."

"I am not," said Simon.

"You are," said Lucy.

"Am not," said Simon.

"Are," said Lucy.

"Not," said Simon.

"CHILDREN!" said Mrs. Mouse.

Grandmother Mouse lived in a house
on the far, far side of the pond.
It was a big pond.
It was a long walk around the pond.

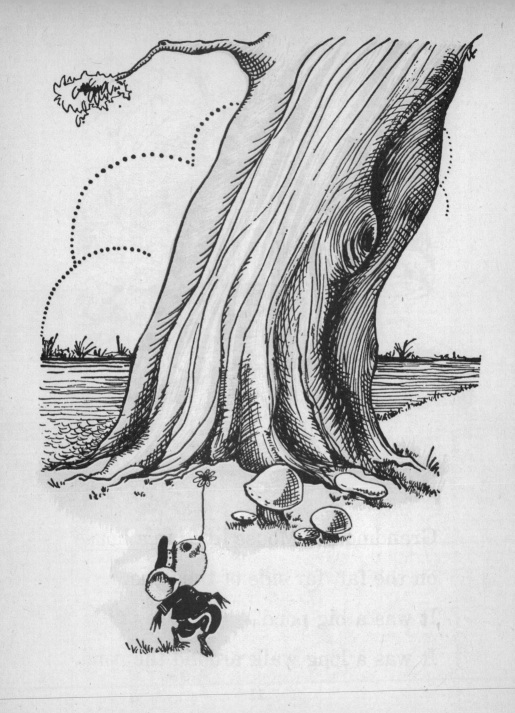

And this is the way they went.

Mrs. Mouse walked first,

then Lucy,

and way in the back

came Simon.

He walked very . . . slowly.

There was Mrs. Frog in the pond.

"Good morning, Mrs. Frog,"

said Mrs. Mouse.

"Say 'good morning,' children."

Lucy said,

"Good morning, Mrs. Frog."

But where was Simon?

Everyone had to wait . . .

and wait. . . .

and wait.

"Hurry up, Simon,"

cried Mrs. Mouse.

"Come over and say 'good morning'

to Mrs. Frog."

At last Simon came.

"Good morning, Mrs. Frog," he said.

"Nice day," said Mrs. Frog.

"We must hurry now,"
said Mrs. Mouse.

"We have a long walk.

Come, Lucy. Hurry up, Simon."

"Yes," said Lucy. "Hurry up, Simon."

"I'm coming," said Simon.

But he stood by the pond.

"Simon, your tail is in the pond,"

said Mrs. Frog.

Simon took a step back.

"Hurry up, Simon,"

cried Mrs. Mouse.

"Yes," said Lucy.

"Hurry up, Simon."

"Indeed!" said Mrs. Frog.

"Hurry up, Simon."

"I'm coming," Simon said.

Then he said good-by to Mrs. Frog.

He walked away very . . . slowly.

But now his tail was wet.

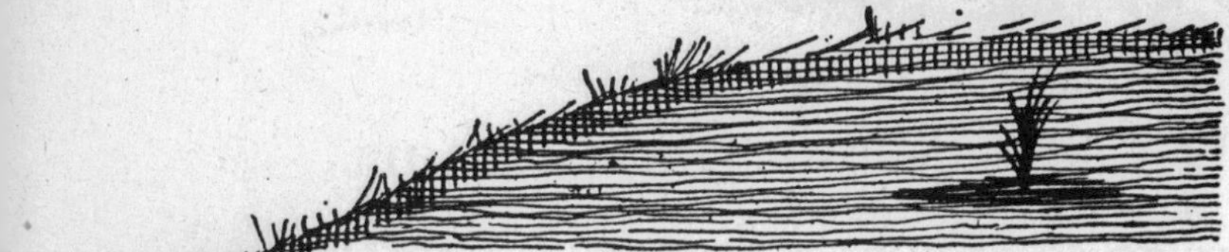

Simon shook his tail.

He shook his tail some more.

There! His tail was dry.

"Hurry up, Simon,"

cried Mrs. Mouse.

"Stay with us."

"Yes," said Lucy. "Stay with us.

You are a cow's tail."

"I am not a cow's tail," Simon said.

"You are," said Lucy.

"I am not," said Simon.

"Are," said Lucy.

"Not," said Simon.

"CHILDREN!" said Mrs. Mouse.

They walked by the side of the

pond—

Mrs. Mouse,

Lucy,

and way in the back

came Simon.

He walked very . . . slowly.

BUMP!

Simon hit his foot.

"Ow!" Simon said.

Then a turtle said,

"Why do you say 'ow'?

You hit your foot on me!"

"I was in a hurry," Simon said.

"In a hurry!" said the turtle.

"You are slower than I am.

I was just walking *past* you."

"Oh," Simon said.

"I must hurry faster, then."

"I think so," said the turtle.

But Simon stood there.

"You are sitting on my tail,"

Simon said.

"Oops!" said the turtle,

and he started to go.

Slowly. . .

Slowly. . .

Slowly.

At last he was off Simon's tail.

Simon said good-by to the turtle.

But now, where was his mother?

And where was his sister?

Simon did not see them.

They had said he must hurry.

They had said he must not be late.

He did not hurry.

And now he was late.

He was a slowpoke.

He was a cow's tail.

He walked by the side of the pond.

It was too late now.

Too late to find his mother
and sister.

Too late to get to Grandmother's.

Too late.

Then Simon saw something
on the pond.

What was it?

It looked like a hat.

It *was* a hat.

It was Lucy's hat.

Lucy had lost her hat!

"I *told* her it was on

upside down," Simon said.

He looked at the hat.

It was just like a little boat.

Simon put one foot in.

Simon put two feet in.

Then he sat down in the hat.

And the hat sailed away.

"I'm sailing a ship," cried Simon.

"I'm sailing a ship on a trip,

oh boy!"

The sun was bright

and the sky was blue.

Simon sat and sailed the hat.

Under the water

Simon saw a fish.

The fish looked up.

The fish said, "Hurry up, Simon."

"It's too late now," Simon said.

"Hold on and sail with me.

I'm sailing a ship on a trip, oh boy!"

And Simon sailed on.

But now there were two—

Simon,

and the fish under the water.

On the water Simon saw a duck.

The duck said, "Hurry up, Simon."

"It's too late now," Simon said.

"Hop in and sail with us.

I'm sailing a ship on a trip, oh boy!"

And Simon sailed on.

But now there were three—

Simon,

the fish,

and the duck on the water.

Over the water Simon saw a bird.

The bird came down

and sat by his side.

The bird said, "Hurry up, Simon."

"It's too late now," Simon said.

"I'm sailing a ship on a trip, oh boy!

You come, too."

And Simon sailed on.

But now there were four—

Simon,

the fish,

the duck,

and the bird over the water.

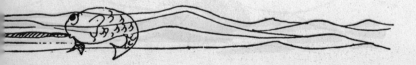

They sailed on and on.

Then Simon said,

"Oh, dear! Lucy will eat

all the cake.

Lucy will drink all the pop.

Lucy will have all the fun

at Grandmother's house.

Just because she is there

and I am not."

"Oh, pish!" said the fish.

"What luck!" said the duck.

"My word!" said the bird.

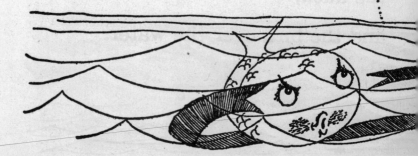

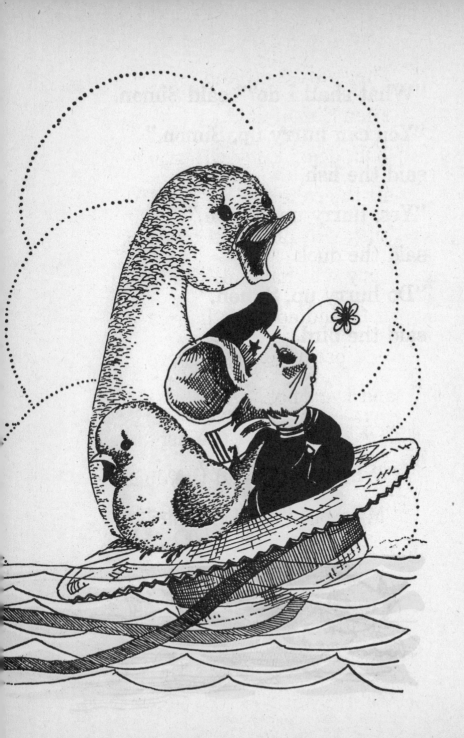

"What shall I do?" said Simon.

"You can hurry up, Simon,"

said the fish.

"Yes, hurry up, Simon,"

said the duck.

"Do hurry up, Simon,"

said the bird.

"But how?" Simon asked.

"I'll push with my fin,"
said the fish.

"I'll push with my bill,"
said the duck.

"I'll push with my feet,"
said the bird.

They all began to push,

and the hat sailed faster,

and faster,

up and down,

over the water.

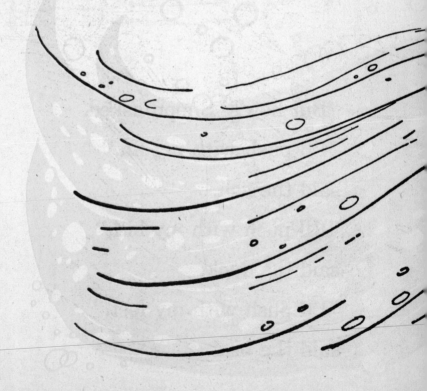

Then—BUMP!

The hat hit the far side

of the pond.

Simon got out, very . . . slowly.

"Good-by," said the fish

under the water.

"Good-by," said the duck

on the water.

"Good-by," said the bird

over the water.

And there was Simon, all alone.

He did not know where he was.

He did not know where

his mother was.

He did not know where

his sister was.

Simon picked up the hat.

He gave the hat a little pat.

Simon walked away

very . . . slowly.

Then he stopped.

What did he smell?

His nose told him.

Simon smelled Grandmother's cake.

Grandmother Mouse lived

in a house

on the far, far side of the pond.

And Simon had sailed

to the far side

of the pond.

To the far, *far* side of the pond.

And there on the hill

was Grandmother's house!

"Grandmother!" Simon cried.

"Save some for me!

I'M HERE! I'M HERE!"

Grandmother Mouse stood

at the door.

"Why, Simon," she said,

"how did you get here so soon?

Where is your mother?

Where is Lucy?"

"I don't know," Simon said.

"They told *me* to hurry."

"Well," said Grandmother,

"have a bite of cake

and we will wait for them."

Simon had five bites of cake.

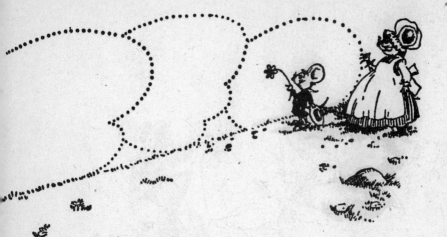

Then Mrs. Mouse and Lucy

came up the hill.

"Why, Simon," said Mrs. Mouse,

"how did you get here

before we did?"

"Yes, Simon," Lucy said, "how

did you get here before we did?"

Simon did not say a thing.

He just held out the hat.

"My hat!" Lucy cried.

"We looked and we looked.

It was nice of you to find it for me."

"Oh, *that!*" said Simon.

"It's my best hat," said Lucy.

"That's all right," said Simon.

"My hat *was* on upside down,"
said Lucy.
"I take back all the bad things
I said."
Simon said, "I take back
all the bad things *I* said."

"No, I said it before you did,"
said Lucy.

"You did not," said Simon.

"I did, too," said Lucy.

"Did not," said Simon.

"Did," said Lucy.

"Not," said Simon.

"CHILDREN!" said Mrs. Mouse.

Grandmother said, "Now, now,
I have cake and pop for everyone.
Come and get it."
"Yes," said Simon, "come
and get it."

"Hurry up, Mother," said Simon.

"Hurry up, Lucy," said Simon.

Mrs. Mouse looked at

Grandmother Mouse.

She said, "See who is saying

'hurry up' now!"